Tell their Story

Robert J. Mueller

C.S.S. Publishing Co., Inc.

Lima, Ohio

Copyright © 1988 by
The C.S.S. Publishing Company, Inc.
Lima, Ohio

Library of Congress Cataloging-in-Publication Data

Mueller, Robert J., 1934-
    Seven tell their story: worship services and monologs for Lent / Robert J. Mueller.
        p.   cm.
    ISBN 1-556-73019-5
    1. Lent. 2. Worship programs.   I. Title.
BV85.M78 1988
264'.4—dc19   87-25954
                                                                                    CIP

8803 / ISBN 1-55673-019-5   PRINTED IN U.S.A.

Table of Contents

<table>
<tr><td>1</td><td># PETER

The Rock
With a Putty Center</td></tr>
</table>

Order of Worship

CALL TO WORSHIP

Leader: We meet here in the name of the Father, and of the Son, and of the Holy Spirit.

People: But out there in the world, it's hard and scary to act as members of God's family.

Leader: Help us, Lord, to be as reckless as Simon Peter in speaking up for you.

People: Help us, Lord, to be wise about our strength, and not to get too friendly with the *enemy*.

All: Forgive us, Lord, when we grumble over last-minute conversions. Instead, help us to share your joy. And when we fail you, look upon us with mercy and take us back again. Amen

HYMN

A RESPONSIVE SHARING OF SIMON PETER'S HISTORY

Leader: Jesus began to teach his disciples that the Son of Man must suffer many things, and be rejected by the elders and chief priests and scribes, and be killed, and after three days rise again.

6

All:	*He said this plainly.*
Females:	And Peter took him, and began to rebuke him.
Males:	But turning and seeing his disciples, he rebuked Peter, and said, "Get behind me, Satan! For you are not on the side of God, but of men."
Leader:	"Simon, Simon, behold, Satan demanded to have you, that he might sift you like wheat."
All:	*"But I have prayed for you that your faith may not fail; and when you have turned again, strengthen your brethren."*
Males:	And Peter said to him, "Lord, I am ready to go with you to prison and to death."
Females:	Jesus said, "I tell you, Peter, the rooster will not crow this day, until you three times deny that you know me."

THE LENTEN MESSAGE
Peter — the Rock With a Putty Center

THE OFFERING

A RESPONSE TO THE LENTEN STORY

Males:	The believer in me says, "I heard God ask, 'Whom shall I send, and who will go for us?' " Then I said, "Here I am! Send me."
Females:	*The unbeliever in me says, "In my last congregation, I got too involved. I'd like to rest for a while now."*
Males:	The believer in me says, "I will share my experience with God with my family. I want them to see that God isn't just back there in history somewhere."
Females:	*The unbeliever in me says, "But my family will think I'm a fanatic. So I'll just watch TV with them."*
Males:	The unbeliever in me says, "My coffee break is not the place to talk about religion."
Females:	*The believer in me says, "I'll listen for cues that my co-workers may have hurts that they'd like to talk about."*

Males: The unbeliever in me says, "Sorry to hear about that. I know how you feel. Would you like to talk to my pastor about that?"

Females: The believer in me says, "Jesus, because we saw you in the sick, the lonely, the hurt, the ones in jail, we were present with them."

Males: The unbeliever in me says, "It's the government's fault. They should not have had all those give-away programs for people who are too lazy to work."

Females: The believer in me says, "God doesn't love us because we are more successful than others. Instead, we want to share the gifts that God has given to us."

All: Lord, give us your Spirit that we may be reckless in sharing ourselves with those who need us, yet be wise enough to know our limits.

HYMN

THE DISMISSAL

Leader: Live joyfully, gratefully, and wisely, by the power of the Holy Spirit, as you share in the death and resurrection of Christ. In the midst of human affairs, be a faithful witness for Christ.

People: **The good and gracious will of God is done indeed without our prayer. But we pray that it will also be done among and by us. Amen**

Suggested Hymns: "Stricken, Smitten, and Afflicted"
"Have Thine Own Way, Lord"
"I Love to Tell the Story"
"Awake, Thou Spirit, Who Didst Fire"
"Faith of Our Brothers" (a revision of "Faith of Our Fathers," made by Brother Andrew. Or, consult Lutheran Bible Translators)

Peter — The Rock With a Putty Center

A Monolog

I am Simon, brother of Andrew, from Galilee. Jesus called me "Rock." You remember me as the disciple who always spoke up, especially that time in the high priest's courtyard when I said I didn't know Jesus. But before you decide about my witness, let me tell my story. Then I have two suggestions for you in your witness for Christ.

To people in Judea, Galileans were second-class Jews. When the Assyrians had destroyed our nothern kingdom about 700 years ago, they brought a lot of foreigners in to settle the country. Some of them married our people, so Galileans today aren't pure-blooded Jews.

Here in Galilee, we don't go in for all the theological hairsplitting of the Scribes and Pharisees. Like them, we're totally serious about God. But we don't try to answer every question there is, nor do we worry too much about keeping their 631 laws. We like to keep some of the mystery about God, yet, as his people, to have a little fun, also.

Most of us in Galilee were surprised when Joseph's son, Jesus, started preaching about repentance and saying that the kingdom of God had come. That was strange talk for a carpenter's son, especially a carpenter from Nazareth.

But the sudden appearance of John the Baptizer caused many people to talk. Here was the son of a priest, dressed like Elijah the prophet, preaching a strange new baptism of repentance. John was calling a proud people to turn their back on everything they valued, and to start a new life with God. By crossing the Jordan and coming to John in foreign territory, the people were symbolically turning their back on what had been precious to them, a kind of "new birth."

John told people that being a child of Abraham meant nothing, that Israel was a dead tree that God was about to chop down. John said God was creating a new people, a people in which race had no meaning at all. You can't imagine how radical John was.

People from Galilee flocked to hear John, like bees after fresh clover. We didn't have much to lose, so we wanted to be in on whatever God was up to. I sure felt weird being immersed in the Jordan River. We Jews had never heard of any kind of baptism. But John said it was time for a radical change. He said we must get ready for God's Anointed One, that his Messiah was already among us. We'd never heard anything like that since Malachi had said, four hundred years ago, that Elijah would come. To me, John was doing just what the prophet had said Elijah would do.

Then one day while John was teaching his disciples, he saw Jesus walking by, and he said to us: "Look at the Lamb of God who takes away the sin of the world!" The next day, John pointed to Jesus and said the same thing. My brother Andrew saw this, and when he told me about it, I said, "That's the signal I've been waiting for. John is telling us to follow the Nazarene, not him!" Andrew and I have been with Jesus ever since that day.

Some of the people Jesus gathered around himself really bothered me. I didn't really like Simon the Zealot. He never said so out loud, but I thought he couldn't wait to stick his dagger in some Roman's gut. Thomas was too cautious. To make him believe anything, you had to show him hard evidence. But Matthew was the real problem. Before Jesus had called him, Matthew had been a tax collector. I couldn't blame him too much for pocketing some of the Roman tax money. But I was ashamed of the people he hung out with. And, as a tax collector, he was actually a traitor to everything we believed in. I couldn't handle it when Jesus chose Matthew as a disciple.

To make matters worse, Matthew threw a big party and invited Jesus and the rest of us. I told Jesus, "Rabbi, you really shouldn't be seen with that crowd!" Jesus got a pained look in his eye. He told me he was going to Matthew's party, and he said we should come, too.

When I told Jesus I wouldn't go, he sat us all down and told a story about a man with two sons. The younger son, Jesus said, demanded his part of his father's property. And after he got it, he went off to a far country, and wasted his inheritance. You know the story. I got the point, too. I was the older son. I was upset because a worthless bum like Matthew had been welcomed back into God' Kingdom. Jesus smiled and said to me: "Simon, you've always been faithful. Everything the Father has is yours. Come, let's rejoice with Matthew. This brother of yours was dead and is alive! He was lost and is found!"

One of my best memories of being with Jesus was the time we left Jewish territory and took a break around Caesarea Philippi. Jesus often checked out what we were learning from him. I never knew exactly how to take some of his questions. That day he asked us, "Who do people say that the Son of Man is?" I knew what Jesus was getting at — he wanted to know who people thought he was. We told him some people thought he was John the Baptizer. We knew John had been killed by King Herod. But a lot of people didn't believe that. Since nobody knew for sure what had happened to that ancient prophet, some people thought Jesus was Elijah. The rare courage of Jesus, yet his cautious approach reminded some folks of the prophet Jeremiah. Others thought Jesus was the prophet Amos, we told him. For once, I thought I knew what Jesus would ask next; he asked, in a quiet but direct voice, "Who do you say I am?" I was ready for that question. I spoke right up, "You are the promised Savior, the Son of God!"

I really didn't understand everything I said. But I knew what Jesus was getting at, and I was completely sure about who he was. As I listened to Jesus and saw what he did, it became clear to me he was God's Anointed One, the person who was everything Israel should be: God's Son. That was a moment I'll never forget.

Another great moment for me was our last Passover meal with Jesus. I knew why Jesus had been so hush-hush about it. We all knew our leaders were going to arrest Jesus the first chance they got. And I wasn't sure that each of the twelve could really be trusted.

When we asked Jessu where he wanted us to prepare the Passover lamb, he told us, "Go into the city, and you will meet a man carrying a jar of water. Follow him . . ." When Jesus said "a man carrying a jar of water," I knew this thing about the upper room had been prearranged. In our culture, men don't carry water jars — that's a woman's job. With the authorities breathing down our necks, Jesus couldn't even tell us where the upper room was. He had to make sure he wasn't arrested there. This wasn't so clear to me then, but it is now.

I felt ashamed of myself that night because we were arguing about who could recline on the left of Jesus. That was the most important place. I was really mad that Judas got that spot. Then Jesus really shamed me by doing the work of a slave and washing our feet. When he came to me, I said, "No! You'll never wash my feet." Jesus had a sad look in his eyes when he told me, "If I don't wash you, you have no share in me." I didn't know what to say. I think I blurted out, "Rabbi, not only my feet but also my hands and my head."

Later in the Passover meal, Jesus was strangely quiet and very upset. Suddenly, he looked at us and said in a firm voice, "One of you is going to betray me!" I had been thinking it might happen, but I still couldn't believe my ears! I motioned to John, who was to the right of Jesus, "Ask him who it is!" I saw John whisper something to Jesus, and then Jesus said something about the next one he would give the sop to. Judas got a strained look on his face, and then he got up and left. I liked Judas, but I wondered what he was up to.

As the Passover meal went on, I forgot about Judas. At one point Jesus took some pieces of unleavened bread, and told us, "Take, eat; this is my body, which is given for you!" Ever since I was a child, I knew the pieces of bread were to remind us that, in Egypt, we rarely had a whole loaf of bread, and that we ate what little we had in great bitterness of heart.

When Jesus said of the bread, "This is me," I got a terrible feeling in my stomach. Did he mean he was soon to feel the broken bitterness of death? "God forbid!" — I almost said out loud.

After we had finished the Passover meal, Jesus took the cup of blessing, gave thanks to God, and said to us: "Drink of this, all of you. This cup is the new covenant in my blood, shed for many to unloose their sins. When you drink of this cup, do it to remember me." That part about the "new covenant in my blood" scared me. I knew that God had promised a new covenant. But a covenant of blood — our Rabbi's blood? Like the broken bread pieces, that sounded like death. But if Jesus is the Messiah, why should he die, I asked myself.

I don't like to tell you what happened next. All of a sudden, I heard Jesus say, "But as I told the Jews . . . so I tell you now, where I'm going, you can't come." I blurted out, "Rabbi, where are you going?" I'd left everything and followed Jesus for almost four years. If he was going somewhere, I wanted to go with him. I remember telling Jesus, "Even if all the others forsake you, I'll never leave you. I'll give my life for you!" It got really quiet in the room when Jesus told me, "I tell you the truth, the rooster will not crow till you've denied me three times."

After all the restless watching and waiting in the Garden of Gethsemane, and the arrest by the mob there, I was in a complete daze. John found me and got me into the high priest's courtyard. He left me sitting by the fire the guards had made to warm themselves. Going in there was my first mistake. If I said too much, my Galilean accent would give me away. But if I moved around too much, some guard or gatekeeper might recognize me. One woman kept saying I had been with the Nazarene. I told her she was crazy. Then one of the guards picked up on my accent. I growled with an oath, "I don't know anything about the guy in there!" Just then, from the direction of Pilate's quarters, I heard a rooster crow. Right then, the guards led Jesus out on the porch. I'll never forget the look he gave me. While it cut me like a sword, Jesus seemed to also say, "I understand, Simon."

I want you to learn at least two lessons from my life with Jesus. First, don't speak out if nobody asked you to. And don't do other people's work for them. If you force your faith on other people, or do most of their work for them, they'll only resent you for it. Be a rock — when you've been invited to, and when the other person is willing to take a risk with you.

The second lesson you can learn from me is to stay out of the *enemy's* camp. I know David killed Goliath, but David wasn't surrounded by the Philistines. My big mistake was to think I could hold my own in the Devil's court. Maybe I could have stood up to one or two of the high priest's guards, but everybody around me was playing on the *enemy's* team. That was too much, even for a Rock like me. So don't try to run with the *enemy*. You'll have to go by their rules, and you'll lose. Be a Rock — know your limits. Don't be a fool, like I was! Fortunately, Jesus looked at me, and brought me to my senses. This time, like in the story he once told, I was the foolish younger son. But Jesus welcomed me back, too. If your "rock" turns to putty, don't forget that!

<table>
<tr><td>2</td><td># CAIAPHAS

To Save
The Nation</td></tr>
</table>

Order of Worship

CALL TO WORSHIP

Leader: We meet here in the name of the Father, and of the Son, and of the Holy Spirit.

People: These words remind us of our Baptism, in which God adopted us into his family.

Leader: Although God invited us into his family, the church has sometimes brought people in by force, and expelled those who rejected its man-made rules.

People: The Scriptures teach that understanding doctrine is not an individual thing, but an issue for the whole body of Christ.

Leader: Yet we have allowed people to publicly distort the Gospel with promises of easy miracles and possibility thinking.

People: We have been more concerned about teaching people a system of belief, than with calling them into a living relationship with God.

Leader: Like the Jewish nation at the time of Christ, the church of our day is badly divided.

People: Like the Dead Sea community, some Christians ignore issues of the day, and talk mainly about saving souls and getting to heaven.

Leader: To avoid upsetting modern ways of thinking, some Christians deny basic teachings of the Bible.

14

People:	**Other Christians say the only way to save our nation is a return to moral living.**
Leader:	The Pharisees and rabbis, at the time of Christ, taught and lived clean lives; but morality didn't save their nation, or make them right with God.
All:	*Forgive us, Lord God, for being more loyal to a church denomination or to the ways of the world, than to you. Give us your Holy Spirit, that we may rightly understand and proclaim your Word, and live as faithful members of your family.*

HYMN

THE SCRIPTURE LESSON John 11:45-53
THE LENTEN MESSAGE *Caiaphas — to Save the Nation*

A RESPONSIVE PRAYER

Leader:	Give us your Holy Spirit, Lord God, that we may rediscover the miracle of your Covenant and of true relationships with our neighbors.
People:	**Keep us from accepting an easy unity that would reject the Gospel, and help us to move beyond church-made religion to your truth.**
Leader:	Where our organizations and customs keep us from being about your saving and uniting work, help us to see this, and to risk changing our selfish and comfortable ways.
People:	**Where we are troubled by the burdens of this sinful world, or threatened by hostile powers, help us to see your presence and care.**
Leader:	As we see the hostile powers uniting in rebellion against you, strengthen your holy people throughout the world with the hope of Christ's victorious return.
All:	*Help us to see, Lord God, that what you give us is not a set of beliefs, but a new relationship with you and with each other. Help your holy people everywhere to rediscover the Gospel and to stand faithfully together as we speak and live out this Good News. Amen*

THE OFFERING

HYMN

THE DISMISSAL

Leader: Live joyfully and gratefully, by the power of the Holy Spirit, as you share in the death and resurrection of Christ. And in the midst of human affairs, make a united witness for Christ.

People: **God tempts no one to sin, but we pray that God would watch over us and keep us so that the devil, the world, and our sinful self may not deceive us and draw us into false belief, despair, and other great and shameful sins. And we pray that even though we are so tempted, we may still win the final victory. Amen**

Suggested Hymns: "Come, Follow Me, the Savior Spake"
"Christ, the Life of All the Living"
"He's Everything to Me"
"Lift High the Cross"

Caiaphas — to Save the Nation

A Monolog

My name is Caiaphas. I was the high priest when our supreme council tried and condemned Yeshua of Nazareth. As the highest leader of God's people, I had the hard job of trying to unite our divided nation, and to work with a foreign power that, at any time, might turn against us and destroy us.

Although I did not grow up in the Holy Land, I believe that we Jews are God's chosen people. I wanted so much to unite our divided nation. I tried to get the Pharisees, the Essenes, and the Sadducees to forget their petty differences, and work together for the good of our nation. But since each group thought only it had the truth, it was hard to get anywhere. The Essenes finally withdrew to the Dead Sea caves and ignored everybody else. At least they weren't going to support the Galilean headhunters! And neither were most of the rabbis. The rabbis dreamed of a kingdom where the Law would someday rule. As for the Galilean rebels, the rabbis said, "Wait and see." Most of the rabbis would neither support nor condemn the Galilean freedom fighters.

Since my own party, the Sadducees, controlled the Temple, and my father-in-law, Annas, a former high priest, was the president of our supreme council, we had a good chance to influence our nation. Because we were reasonable people, we had a chance to both unite our nation, and to work out some kind of relationship with the Roman government. Since my father-in-law, Annas, controlled the sale of sacrificial animals in the Temple, and the money-changers there, we had the money to influence people in Rome. The government in Rome might laugh at our religion of one God, but they listened to our money!

As I said, the only group that worried me was the Galilean freedom fighters. They could not be bought off by our money, nor scared off by our council rulings against them.

I had recently taken office when I picked up a new rumor from Galilee. A carpenter's son from Nazareth was attracting a lot of attention. Like John the Baptizer, he seemed very critical of the religion taught by our rabbis. Unlike our rabbis, he did not back up his teaching by quoting the ancient teachers. From what my informers told me, this man seemed to be a new Moses and another Solomon. He claimed to have new insight into what the Mount Sinai Covenant really meant. Worse yet, he reportedly said that, in himself, the Rule of God had come on earth. I smelled a political rat in that kind of talk!

It bothered me, too, that the Nazarene had twelve close followers mostly from Galilee, and that he was attracting a lot of attention all over Palestine. My informers said several leading rabbis secretly believed in him, and even some members of our supreme council openly spoke out in his favor.

I didn't pay much attention to the reports that the Nazarene healed people from all kinds of diseases, and that he allegedly fed over five thousand people from five barley loaves and two boiled fish. That bread and fish story sounded too much like the old myths about manna and quails in the desert. Only the fanatics in Galilee and the half-breeds in Samaria believed those old desert yarns.

The Nazarene did cause quite a fuss when, early in his public life, he literally threw the sacrifice sellers and the money-changers out of the Temple. My father-in-law, Annas, was really mad about that. But he couldn't arrest the Nazarene, because the people deeply resented our control of the Temple bazaar, and saw the Nazarene as a real hero. Although I wasn't sure at first what to make of him, the Nazarene was clearly a man we had to watch.

What he was up to became painfully clear to me when, on the first day of Passover week, the Nazarene rode into Jerusalem on a mule. I didn't have to be a Bible expert to see that the Nazarene was applying the ancient word of Zechariah to himself. By riding in procession into the Holy City on a mule — the animal our kings had always used as a symbol of their peaceful intentions, the Nazarene was saying, I am Israel's true King. You must give your complete loyalty to me!

When I heard what the Nazarene had done, and how the whole Passover crowd was calling him the Son of David, I called a meeting of the religious leaders in Jerusalem. We all knew something had to be done, and done quickly. Although the Roman Procurator, Pontius Pilate, had brought extra troops with him from Caesarea, they could not control the Passover crowds — if the Nazarene called for open rebellion against us and against Rome.

As I expected, the other leaders said they didn't know what to do. They knew the Nazarene had to be stopped. But they were afraid to take a definite stand. I finally told them, "There can be no compromise with the Nazarene now. It's either us or him. If we want to save our beloved nation, we must destroy the prophet from Nazareth. It's a dangerous step to take, I know. But we cannot allow open rebellion in Jerusalem and the risk that Rome will then come in and destroy us all. Killing the Nazarene is the lesser of two evils." My colleagues, even though they were from different parties, agreed with me: the Nazarene must die.

However, since the Nazarene was so secret about where he stayed — except when he taught each day in the Temple — I had no idea how to get him arrested. My informers couldn't find out where he was staying at night that week. After he taught every day in the Temple, he would seem to just vanish at sundown.

My problem was solved in a way I'd never dreamed of! One of his closest friends, a man from Kerioth in Judea, played right into our hands. Because I couldn't figure out what he was up to, I didn't trust Judas. But he agreed to help us arrest the Nazarene secretly, so the crowds wouldn't know what happened until it was too late. I got Pilate to write an order for the Nazarene's arrest, and I used our temple security people to help Pilate's soldiers arrest the fanatic from Galilee.

Judas told us that his rabbi was celebrating the Passover with his followers in the upper room of one of Jerusalem's prominent citizens. But when our detachment got there, the Nazarene had already left. It looked like he had slipped away from us again. But then Judas remembered that his rabbi often went up to the Mount of Olives, to a garden that a local ruler allowed him to use. That's where my people arrested the troublesome rabbi from Nazareth.

I had already alerted the members of our supreme council to be ready for a quick meeting to plan how we could get the Roman Procurator to order the Nazarene's execution. I didn't intend to have a formal trial — we didn't have the authority to pass the death sentence, anyway. I only wanted to firm up charges that would force Pontius Pilate to order the Nazarene's death. Pilate could be hard to deal with. But he had made several big political mistakes, and if we threatened again to report him to Emperor Tiberius, which we had done once, I knew Pilate would do what we told him to.

The hearing I had for the Nazarene didn't go too well. The witnesses I had called to testify couldn't tell their stories the same way. The Nazarene didn't even have to answer those fools! I tried to ask him about his public teaching, but the Nazarene knew that, in Jewish law, it is illegal to ask a person to testify against himself. The Nazarene simply said he'd always taught in public, that I should cross-examine my fellow Jews who heard him teach in the Temple. He had me on that one!

I finally asked the Nazarene a question I knew he'd have to answer. I put him under oath, and asked him, "Are you the Anointed One, the Son of God?" I knew something about what the Nazarene had claimed to be — that only he, not the people of Israel, is God's Servant or Son. I knew that if the Nazarene would repeat his claim before our supreme council, I had his life in my hands; and my nit-picking colleagues would unite to condemn the Nazarene to death.

The Nazarene's answer, though both he and I knew what he had to say, shocked even me! He said that not only were my words about him true, but that the time is coming when we will see him "seated at the right hand of Power, and coming on the clouds of heaven." (Matthew 26:64)

When the Nazarene said he would come on the clouds of heaven, he meant that he, one human being, is the true Israel, the true Servant or Son of God. When he said we would see him seated at the right hand of Power, he clearly made himself divine! Although I knew what he had to say, I could hardly believe the Nazarene had so clearly condemned himself. There was no question about it; such a madman must die! And die he did.

Although we had risked the anger of the people, most of them didn't find out about the death sentence until it was too late. The Nazarene's followers were so shocked that most of them simply melted away. They made no attempt to excite the Passover crowd against us. We had put out the word that crucifixion awaited anyone who publicly claimed to support the Nazarene. That stopped even the Galilean hotheads from doing anything at the time.

The clear-cut stand against the Nazarene united the various parties of our religion as never before. True, it was only an agreement against something. But I had hopes that, from now on, we could work together on positive things. The main thing was that I had acted firmly to head off another ill-fated revolt against Rome, which could only spill a lot of Jewish blood and destroy our beloved nation. The fanatics were still there, but the Nazarene would not lead them to bring in his misguided notion about the Rule of God.

Like the naive fools before him, the rabbi from Nazareth would soon be forgotten. Our beloved nation was moving toward unity, and we could learn to live safely with the Roman government. As high priest, I had helped save the nation.

3 | # JUDAS
A Question Of Power

Order of Worship

CALL TO WORSHIP

Leader: We meet here in the name of the Father, and of the Son, and of the Holy Spirit.

People: These words remind us of our Baptism, in which we received new life to follow God's way.

Leader: As God's new creation, we live not for ourselves, but for others, especially for the weak and hopeless neighbor.

People: We meet here to remember Jesus, who willingly became the Lamb of God, the innocent and perfect sacrifice for our sins.

All: Lord, you do not need us to make your Kingdom come. But give us your Spirit that we may be used to bring strength and hope to our weak and dying world.

HYMN

A RESPONSIVE READING OF PSALM 41

Lectern side: Blessed is he who considers the poor! The Lord delivers him in the day of trouble;

Pulpit side: The Lord protects him and keeps him alive; he is called blessed in the land; thou dost not give him up to the will of his enemies.

Lectern side:	The Lord sustains him on his sickbed; in his illness thou healest all his infirmities.
Pulpit side:	**As for me, I said, "O Lord, be gracious to me; heal me, for I have sinned against thee!"**
Lectern side:	My enemies say of me in malice: "When will he die, and his name perish?"
Pulpit side:	**And when one comes to see me, he utters empty words, while his heart gathers mischief; when he goes out, he tells it abroad.**
Lectern side:	All who hate me whisper together about me; they imagine the worst for me.
Pulpit side:	**They say, "A deadly thing has fastened upon him; he will not rise again from where he lies."**
Lectern side:	Even my bosom friend in whom I trusted, who ate of my bread, has lifted his heel against me.
Pulpit side:	**But do thou, O Lord, be gracious to me, and raise me up, that I may requite them!**
Lectern side:	By this I know that thou art pleased with me, in that my enemy has not triumphed over me.
Pulpit side:	**But thou hast upheld me because of my integrity, and set me in thy presence for ever.**
All:	***Blessed be the Lord, the God of Israel, from everlasting to everlasting! Amen***

THE SCRIPTURE LESSON   Matthew 26:14-25; 27:1-5

THE LENTEN MESSAGE   *Judas — a Question of Power*

OFFERING

A RESPONSE TO THE LENTEN STORY

Lectern side:	God tells us, "If you are willing to learn, willing to be taught, you will become great in my Kingdom."
Pulpit side:	**The world tells us, "The way to be somebody is to look out for yourself. After all, nobody else will."**

Lectern side:	God says, "When you are weak, then you have true strength."
Pulpit side:	**The world says, "If you don't assert yourself, you'll never have anything. You can't let people walk over you."**
Lectern side:	God says, "All things work together for good for those who love me."
Pulpit side:	**The world says, "Decide for yourself what is good and what is not good. If you can, avoid anything painful."**
Lectern side:	God says, "Your value and dignity come from what I say you are."
Pulpit side:	**The world says, "Your value depends on what you do, or on what other people think you are worth."**
All:	*The way of God is self-denial. Only self-denial leads to life. The world's way is self-assertion. It leads to death, to separation from God. Lord, help us to choose life! Amen*

HYMN

THE PRAYERS

THE DISMISSAL

Leader:	Live joyfully and gratefully, by the power of the Holy Spirit, as you share in the death and resurrection of Christ. In the midst of human affairs, be a patient witness for Christ.
People:	**The Kingdom of God comes indeed without our prayer, of itself. But we pray that it may also come to us, and through us. Amen**

Suggested Hymns: "Lord, as Thou Wilt, Deal Thou with Me"
"I Gave My Life for Thee"
"Pass It On" (It Only Takes a Spark)

Judas

A Question of Power

I am Judas, from Kerioth in Judea. I was one of the Christ's first disciples. To you my name means betrayal, the son of Satan who turned Jesus over to his enemies. But before you pass sentence on me, listen to what I have to say. Then we'll see if you do any better than I did.

I was the only disciple Jesus chose from Judea. The rest were from Galilee, and most of them were related to each other. The other disciples were jealous of me. Except for Matthew, I was the only disciple with a formal education. Jesus knew I could handle money. That's why he made me treasurer of our group.

The way Jesus chose us was very unusual. Normally, if a young man wanted to learn from a rabbi, you had to ask him to let you be his student. Jesus did just the opposite. He asked us to be his disciples.

Like the other eleven, I was strongly attracted to Jesus. He didn't try to impress people by how many great rabbis of the past he could quote. He would tell us, "You have heard that it was said — but I say unto you . . . !" When Jesus spoke, it was like Elijah single-handedly taking on the prophets of Baal. With one short statement, Jesus would burn up all the drivel of this or that ancient rabbi.

In Jesus, I saw a man with authority, a man who would stand up to evil no matter what. In his fearless stand, he reminded me of Mattathias, who had taken a lonely stand against Antiochus Epiphanes. Antiochus was the Syrian king who had tried to destroy our Jewish way of life about 200 years ago. Once, an ambassador from Antiochus had given the village where Mattathias lived an ultimatum — either swear loyalty to Antiochus and adopt the Greek culture, or else! When one Jewish man from the village stepped forward to accept the ambassador's offer, Mattathias killed the man on the spot. He called Israel to defend the pure religion, and to rally with him in the hills. Later, although his son Judas was killed in battle, after several great victories over Antiochus, his son John drove the Syrian devil out of the country and restored our freedom. The people who rallied around Mattathias were called the "Pure

Ones." This group of fiercely loyal Jews later became the Pharisees of my time.

I saw Jesus as one of these "Pure Ones," a man completely dedicated to God, a man like Mattathias, and Elijah, who was not afraid to stand alone against great odds.

And Jesus had more than rare courage and conviction. I also saw great power in him. Not only did he take a little boy's lunch of five barley loaves and two fish, and feed more than five thousand people, even the demons had to obey him. Mary of Magdala was living proof of that.

I'll never forget meeting that funeral procession from the city of Nain. It was about mid-morning. A large crowd went along with us. The disciples were worn out from going through the villages to tell them Jesus was coming. It hadn't been easy, because a lot of people were sick and tired of messiah-talk. Several frauds had appeared lately. By saying that Yahweh had called them to overthrow the hated Romans, they had gained quite a following. But Rome had reacted with brutal force. In Galilee, the hotbed for rebellion, a thousand rebels were hung on trees along the highways. When Jesus said, "If anyone wants to be my disciple . . . he must take up his *cross* every day," we knew what he meant!

As we came near the city gate of Nain, we were hoping for a little rest. Then out came this funeral procession. The dead man was the only son of his widowed mother. We waited helplessly for the mourners to walk on by. We hoped Jesus would ignore them, and let us go into town. After all, we said, it's too late to do anything for the widow's son now.

I was surprised when Jesus, tired as he was, stopped the procession, and said to the widow, "Don't cry." I couldn't believe it when he walked up to the open coffin and touched it. No rabbi would have done that. To touch the dead made the rabbi unclean, unable to worship with the community until that evening. "What's Jesus up to?" we wondered. Then he said to the dead boy, "Young man, I tell you, wake up!" I couldn't believe my eyes when the dead man sat up and started to talk! I'd never seen anything like that in my whole life! Neither had anybody else! I'd read about Elijah restoring the widow's son to life, but that was a long time ago, and I wondered how true all that stuff really was. But I had seen Jesus raise the widow of Nain's son with my own eyes. And hundreds of other people had seen it, too! This clinched it for me. "Jesus really is the Messiah," I said to myself. "There's no stopping him now!"

What Jesus did in that final entry into Jerusalem also impressed me. We all knew about the prophecy of Zechariah that our Messiah would ride into Jerusalem on a donkey. This would be the signal that the Day of the Lord had come, that Yahweh would personally act to save his people and destroy our enemies.

When Jesus rode a donkey into Jerusalem that day, he was sending a clear message to our leaders — that he was Israel's King, the great Son of David whom Yahweh had promised to send to rule his people forever.

I really got excited when Jesus threw the money-changers and the sacrifice-peddlers out of the Temple. It looked like Jesus was really going to take control. He was finally making public use of his power. But then, instead of openly and clearly saying he was the Anointed One, calling the faithful to rally around him, and declaring war on wicked Rome, Jesus taught quietly in the Temple all that week, and retreated each night to Bethany.

Suddenly, Jesus seemed so secretive, remote, and different. Instead of calling the faithful to unite around him, to take up a holy war against the Roman harlot, Jesus talked more about his death, the Time of Trouble and the End of the Age.

He seemed to sense that I was deeply confused about him. He would look at me and talk about a man doomed by the devil. When Mary poured all that expensive perfume on him, I said the perfume should have been sold and the money given to the poor. Jesus knew what I was trying to say, but he praised Mary's act as preparing him for his burial! "What kind of talk is that for the Son of David?" I wondered. Where is the man who once said, "All things have been delivered to me by my Father"? If, as he had shown, he had power over both the devil and death, why wasn't he using it now? What kind of madness was he leading us into? Why had he suddenly become so secretive and so morbid?

I finally couldn't take it anymore. To me, Jesus seemed as phony as all those who had recently deluded us. At least, they had led people to fight against Rome! It seemed all Jesus talked about was his own absurd death. This delusion had to stop, I said. So I went to the authorities and agreed to make sure they could arrest Jesus quietly. Maybe I thought that would force him to use the power I knew he had. I knew it was a terrible, desperate act. But I didn't see any other way out. The people of God deserved a real Son of David, not a death-wish madman from Galilee!

After Jesus was arrested like a common criminal in the Garden of Gethsemane, and illegally tried and condemned by the Supreme Council — by men who were supposed to be our great spiritual leaders — I saw I had committed the unpardonable sin. I couldn't stand the pain of that guilt.

My life with Jesus raises some questions about yours. For you, Jesus is Lord, but what does he do for you when your doctor says you have a terminal illness? What's your feeling when your college-bound son, who has several large scholarships and a brilliant future ahead, is killed by a drunk driver? How do you feel then about your "almighty" Lord?

How do you handle it when your enemies, who are often openly wicked, get the upper hand over you? Do you really believe that talk about "Love your enemies," "Bless those who persecute you," or "Repay evil with good"? Don't you instead hope and even pray that God would strike your enemies dead, or otherwise take care of them? Be honest, now! How do you feel when your enemies prosper, while you suffer? How do you feel then about your "almighty" Lord?

If you really believe that you should repay evil with good, how do you explain that you have "converted" many of your enemies by force, and killed innocent people in the name of truth? If your Lord is really "almighty," then why do you so often take things into your own hands?

Like me, when the Nazarene doesn't meet your expectations, do you betray him, too? The price they paid me to betray Jesus — thirty pieces of silver — was the price to redeem a slave. What's the price for you?

Unlike me, perhaps you will not only see your guilt, but also throw yourself upon God's mercy. But have you really faced the enormity of your guilt? Don't kid yourself — a "canned" confession from a hymnbook doesn't accomplish it! You've got to be real about yourself.

I didn't see it, but the unpardonable sin is to reject God's mercy. As the Master said, "Whoever comes to me, I will not turn him away." I wish I could have believed that. But it's not too late for you!

<table>
<tr><td>4</td><td>

PONTIUS PILATE

*Taking Care
Of Business*

</td></tr>
</table>

Order of Worship

CALL TO WORSHIP

Leader: We meet here in the name of God — Father, Son, and Holy Spirit.

People: These words remind us of our Baptism, in which we died with Christ, and were raised with him to be about our Father's business.

Leader: We could be many other places, but we chose to remember Christ's command to come together, and to encourage our fellow believers.

People: We meet to reflect upon the meaning of Christ's suffering and death for our lives today.

All: Lord, give us your Spirit, that despite the cost, we may act justly ourselves and seek justice for others. With your Spirit, help us to back up what we say about you with faithful action. Amen

HYMN

SCRIPTURE LESSON　　　　　　　John 18:26 — 19:16

THE LENTEN MESSAGE　　　　*Taking Care of Business*

A REFLECTION UPON PILATE AND THE PEOPLE OF GOD

Leader: As procurator of the Roman province of Judea, Pontius Pilate had a special privilege and responsibility.

People: **As people whom the Holy Spirit has shown the truth of God, we have a special privilege and responsibility.**

Leader: For Pilate, it was important to make a name for himself, to be remembered in history as a great man.

People: **God has given us a name — his children and inheritors of eternal life. Because of Jesus, the Expected Deliverer, God remembers us today and always.**

Leader: For Pilate, authority meant power to get people to do what he wanted.

People: **As people of God, our authority is to serve and to help people, even as Christ stoops down to help us.**

Leader: For Pilate, justice was not as important as survival, at any cost.

People: **By his innocent suffering and death as a criminal, Jesus shows us that doing God's will is more important than survival.**

Leader: As a person trained in Roman law, Pontius Pilate knew what was right, but he did not act on that knowledge.

People: **Help us, Lord, to back up our good words with faithful action, that people may see your truth and love in our lives.**

All: *Lord, in your undeserved love, you made us members of God's family. Give us your Spirit, that we may faithfully carry out this great privilege and responsibility. Help us to see that our calling is to do God's will, and to believe that nothing will separate us from God's love. Amen*

THE OFFERING

HYMN

THE PRAYERS

THE BENEDICTION
Leader: The God of peace brought back from the dead our Lord Jesus, who by his blood made an everlasting Covenant to become the great King. May he give you every good thing you need, to do what he wants you to do, working in us through Jesus Christ what pleases him.

People: **The good and gracious will of God is done indeed without our prayer, but we pray that it will be done among us also. To him be glory forever. Amen**

Suggested Hymns: "Savior, When in Dust to You"
"When I Survey the Wondrous Cross"
"Take Time to Be Holy"

Pontius Pilate — Taking Care of Business

A Monolog

My name is Pontius Pilate. I am the procurator of the Roman province of Judea, in Palestine. When I tried your "king," you probably think that I made a mockery out of justice, and that I took the easy way out. But let me tell my story. Then we'll see how seriously you ake the claims of your "king."'

I was appointed procurator over this tough Roman province in the twenty-sixth year of your movement, and I served nine years. To some Romans, Palestine is the last place on earth they'd want to live. I wasn't wild about it, but representing Rome in Judea was a great challenge. And for the Caesar to give me this sensitive job meant he had a lot of confidence in me.

One good thing about ruling Judea was that my headquarters was in Caesarea, on the seacoast. Caesarea was a nicer, more modern town than Jerusalem, and the folks in Caesarea weren't a bunch of religious freaks.

Of course, I made many visits to Jerusalem — to try special criminals, to make deals with the Sadducees who controlled the Temple and the Supreme Council, and to remind *King* Herod that, in Judea, I had the real power.

I never kept it a secret that I thought Jews are lower than swine. They gave Caesar what was his, but they were always plotting some kind of rebellion. I've got solid evidence that their rabbis teach people to pray for the "Day of the Lord," when their god will blast us Romans off the earth. That'll take troops, and that means rebellion!

Things got tense every year at their Passover. Thousands of fanatical Jews from Palestine and all over the world gathered in Jerusalem to remember that myth about being set free from the Pharaoh in Egypt. What pious drivel! The Jews will never be free again. Rome will rule them — and the rest of the world — forever!

The first time I visited Jerusalem, I said I'd show those Jews who's boss. When the guards of the other procurators had come into the old city, they had taken off the standards on top of their flags. The standards were a small image of the current Roman Emperor. As you may know, the Jews are not allowed to make or have any kind of images. And since we call our Emperor a "god," the Jews always objected to the standards as idolatry.

I said to myself, "I don't care what the other Roman officials have done. I'm going to put those fanatics in their place!" I knew the Jews would scream idolatry, but my units carried their standards right next door to the Temple.

I hate to admit it, but I misjudged the Jewish leaders. Not only did their supreme council issue a formal protest, some of the leaders followed me all the way back to Caesarea; and they hounded me about the standards for five days after that! I finally agreed to meet with them in the amphitheatre. Then I surrounded them with Roman troops and told them to shut up, or I'd order my troops to cut off their heads on the spot. I couldn't believe it — most of them exposed their necks to my soldiers, and said, "Start cutting!" I had to give in. My get-tough policy backfired on me.

Later on, I thought that if I did the Jews a big favor, I could win them over. Since Jerusalem had always had a water problem, I decided to build a new waterline into the city. But the problem was: where could I get the extra money? I couldn't raise taxes. Too many of my tax collectors were already dying from zealot-poisoning — a dagger in the ribs!

Then I learned that the Temple had a lot of money in a little-known fund that the priests didn't ordinarily use. The money had been given for questionable reasons, and sometimes by the wrong kind of people. In raiding this special fund of the Temple, I solved the priests' conscience problem, and got the extra money I needed.

I thought the Jewish people would be tickled pink with the new waterline. But the people didn't buy it at all. When they found out that I had used money from their temple, they protested and started riots all over Jerusalem. I had backed down before, but I wasn't going to this time! I sent my troops out into the crowds disguised as Jews, and, upon my signal, they clubbed the rioters down like gnats. A lot of Jews met their creator that day!

I didn't give up; but neither did the stupid Jews. To show my loyalty to and my appreciation for Tiberius Caesar, I had some special shields made for my guard units, and I had the Emperor's name engraved on them. When I visited Jerusalem, my guards naturally placed these shields in the old palace of the Herods next to the Temple. However, the Jewish Supreme Council asked me to remove them. They rattled off the usual rubbish that, since the shields were dedicated to a man we laughingly called a "god," they were a direct insult to their "true God."

"The shields stay," I said. But the Jews went over my head. They reported me to Tiberius, and the Emperor told me to get rid of the shields, or else. I got the message. The Jews had beaten me again!

I know more about the rabbi from Nazareth than you may think. Almost from the beginning, my sources kept me informed of where he was and what he was saying. What he was saying was clearly no threat to Rome. But the Jewish leaders were right — the Nazarene was a threat to them! To Jesus, the devil was not Rome. The devil, he said, was the Jewish leaders and their man-made theology. I wasn't all that interested, but I did wonder how the Supreme Council would handle the Nazarene troublemaker.

The Sadducees surprised me when they had some of their temple police secretly arrest Jesus during the Passover. I understand one of the Nazarene's closest friends tipped them off where to find him one night, away from all the Passover crowds. I admired the Jewish leaders' courage. When they realized it was either the Nazarene or them, they took care of the problem!

But why did they ask me to do their dirty work for them? They didn't have the legal authority to execute Jesus, but that hadn't stopped them from trying to stone him to death several times before. When the Supreme Council voted unanimously to execute Jesus, why didn't they quietly kill him off themselves? Why bring their stupid religious problems to me?

When the Jewish leaders mentioned Galilee, I got an idea. Since the accused was from Herod's territory, why not let the old half-Jew decide about Jesus! I knew that ever since Herod had killed John the Baptizer, he had really been paranoid. My sources said that when Herod heard about all the alleged miracles Jesus was doing, the old fox really thought John had come back to life again. I can hear Herod telling the Nazarene, "Prove to me that you're no fool — walk across my swimming pool!"

But, as I should have known, Herod didn't get anything out of Jesus. He mocked the Jewish leaders by sending the Nazarene back to me, wearing a kingly robe. Herod was saying, "That's the kind of wretched *king* you Jews deserve!"

Whatever the Nazarene had allegedly said or done, I couldn't care less. I was intrigued, though, by their charge that he claimed to be a king. But even if he had, he was obviously insane. Some of his close followers were known zealots — the people who stuck daggers in my tax collectors. But Jesus had no real following, and he was never known to have said anything against Caesar.

By asking the Jews to choose between the harmless Nazarene and cutthroat Barabbas, I hoped to get myself out of a jam. I knew that if I didn't pacify the Jews in this case, they'd report me to Tiberius again, and my days as procurator would be over. I got the message, but I almost spit in their faces when the Jewish leaders said, "We have no king but Caesar!"

I knew my wife had been talking to some of the Nazarene's people, but I couldn't believe it when, right when I was cross-examining Jesus, she sent someone to tell me, "Let that righteous man alone. I suffered much in a dream last night on account of him." (Matthew 27:19, Beck) "Fate of the gods!" I said to myself. "Even my wife is caught up in this superstition about the Nazarene!"

I can't live by superstition. What I had to do was clear. Let the stupid Jews have their way with the fool from Nazareth. He seemed to want to die — so why not let him! What's one religious freak, compared to my being the great procurator of Judea? My survival is more important than the ideas of some Galilean madman.

I suppose you people say that I'm a disgrace to the Roman system of justice. But before you condemn me, ask yourself, "In my society, what carries more weight: justice, or what big business and big money want? When I see something wrong being done, if the wrongdoer writes out my paycheck or otherwise has control over me, do I speak out? It's easy to say the right thing should be done, but, if speaking out for the truth will cost me personally, do I insist that justice be done?"

I can hear you folks saying that I took the easy way out, that I should not have caved in to the threats of the Jewish leaders. Again, before you condemn me, ask yourself, "When I face hard questions, do I say, "Oh, that's a political question! We can't discuss that as religious people. Religion must stick to saving souls." I understand the Nazarene once said that if you want to save your life, you must lose it— for him. How many of you folks really believe that? I think that most of you, like me, take the easy way out. You're serious about religion, but it's mostly just ceremony and stuff in your head. You don't really use it where you live every day. Because peace and harmony are more important than doing the will of your God, you work only with folks who agree with you. Like me, don't you take the easy way out?

I got my slam in against the Jews when I marked the cross of the Nazarene: "Jesus of Nazareth, King of the Jews." He was the only kind of king those fools will ever have!

The Jewish leaders didn't like the title I put on the Nazarene's cross. You folks say the Nazarene is your king. If so, how seriously do you take his claims? If you were arrested on suspicion of being a Christian, would there be enough evidence to convict you?

5 | # BARABBAS
A Safe Terrorist

Order of Worship

CALL TO WORSHIP

Leader: We meet here in the name of God — Father, Son, and Holy Spirit.

People: These words remind us of our Baptism, in which we were marked with the Cross, a sign of death.

Leader: As followers of Christ, we are called to take real risks, to be and do what popular religion and the government may condemn.

People: In the life and death of Christ, we see that the enemy is not out there somewhere, but in our own sinful pride.

All: Give us your Spirit, Lord God, that we may obey Christ in all that we do, and not confuse who our real enemy is. Amen

HYMN

SCRIPTURE LESSON   Matthew 27:15-26

THE LENTEN MESSAGE   *Barabbas — a Safe Terrorist*

A REFLECTION ON JESUS AND BARABBAS

Leader: Jesus says, "Happy are those who are poor in spirit."

People: Barabbas says, "Humility is a sign of weakness. If you don't grab what you want, you'll never make it."

Leader: Jesus says, "Happy are those who mourn."

People: Barabbas says, "It's silly to cry over what we've lost. I'm looking out for what I can get."

Leader: Jesus says, "Happy are those who are gentle."

People: Barabbas says, "Nice guys finish last! If people won't move over, move over them!"

Leader: Jesus says, "Happy are those who hunger and thirst for right relationships."

People: Barabbas says, "Who cares about how others feel about me? I know what I need."

Leader: Jesus says, "Happy are those who are merciful."

People: Barabbas says, "Give people an inch, and they'll take a mile."

Leader: Jesus says, "Happy are those who make peace."

People: Barabbas says, "I'll get my friends together, and we'll make a believer out of that guy!"

Leader: Jesus says, "Happy are those who are persecuted for doing right."

People: Barabbas says, "I'm not going to promote any lost causes."

All: *To follow Jesus is a real risk. But it gives us joy and wholeness. To be like Barabbas also takes courage. But Barabbas is not calling for anything new, and he keeps us from seeing who the real enemy is. Give us your Spirit, Lord God, that we may obey Christ in all that we do. Amen*

THE OFFERING

HYMN

THE DISMISSAL

Leader: Live joyfully and boldly, as you share in Christ's death and resurrection. In the power of his Spirit, take real risks for Jesus.

People: We do not ask God to take us out of our dangerous world, but that he would keep us faithful as

we resist the Devil, the world, and our own sinful desires. Lord Jesus, the Expected Deliverer, have mercy on us! Amen

Suggested Hymns: "When I Survey the Wondrous Cross"
"Were You There"
"The Son of God Goes Forth to War"

Barabbas — a Safe Terrorist

A Monolog

Although most of you don't know me personally, you know something about me. You know that I have the reputation of being a radical — that whatever the system is, I'm against it!

I'm not here to change your thinking about me, or to explain how I got to be who I am. I'm here to ask a question that both you and I need to answer, "Why me instead of him?"

My name is Barabbas. I'm the one the crowd chose instead of the rabbi from Nazareth. Barabbas — my name means: "son of a father," that is, of a rabbi, a teacher. Isn't it ironic? My name means "son of a father," while the Nazarene said he is the Son of our Father — God. But why did people choose me, instead of him?

I knew the Nazarene well. We both grew up in Galilee. We both loved the old-time religion of Moses, Elijah, and David. Like most Galileans, we felt the only good Roman was a dead one. We also thought that our southern neighbors, the Samaritans, were a bunch of prejudiced snobs. They were still rehashing the old war over whether we should worship in Jerusalem or at Bethel.

After Jesus left Nazareth, I didn't see much of him. I heard he joined up with some desert hermit named John. I left Cana and joined one of the hill country gangs. We didn't do anything bad — at first. We sawed off the spokes in the wheels of Roman chariots, and stole horses from Pilate's compound in Caesarea. Then we started raiding the small towns of Judea. The local yokels couldn't catch us — not that they really wanted to! And we'd hide out in the hills until everything cooled off. But we finally went too far. We tried to raid King Herod's desert hide-out east of the Dead Sea. We got into Herod's castle with no problems, but then a guard saw us. One of our guys panicked and knifed the guard. Most of us got away, but Herod's police tracked me down. I got sentenced for murder and for trying to overthrow the government by force. Only a half-Jew like Herod could have such a warped sense of justice!

Like I said, I didn't see much of Jesus after he left Nazareth. I heard he went around preaching and teaching what the Old Covenant really meant. And I heard he healed all kinds of sick people, that he even raised a guy in Bethany from the dead. Well, I really think all that healing stuff is just a bunch of messiah-talk. And we've had several phony messiahs lately. Trouble is, these expected deliverers have a bloody habit of ending up on a Roman cross.

Jesus was just a traveling teacher. Although he said our leaders were like whitewashed tombs, and that Yahweh is our Lord, not any Caesar, he didn't get involved in any kind of politics. While a lot of people supported him — even some people in high places — he didn't seem to know who he really was. He didn't seem to be the kind of guy that anybody would want killed.

But when I look at myself, when I look at other people, I think I know why they wanted me, instead of him. For one thing, I didn't require anything of people. I appealed strictly to people's self-interest. I appealed to people's prejudice, fear, suspicion, fantasy — things they wanted, but didn't really need.

The Nazarene did just the opposite. He required something of people. He called people to repent, to change — both their attitudes and their behavior. He said we can't say that we love God and then turn away from our neighbor. He said the rule of God is not back there in the good old days of David and Solomon, nor in the wonderful world of tomorrow. He said the rule of God is here and now — in him!

Now that's scary stuff! I like to think that I've already got everything worked out, that I'm in control of my life, that I'll decide who deserves my help. I'm not going to believe that wild stuff about finding my life by losing it!

I can see why people — then and now — choose me instead of him. Even though I am a terrorist, I don't really require anything new of people. He did — and still does. That's one reason why people choose me instead of him.

I think another reason why people choose me is because we don't like to know who the real enemy is.

It's true that, in asking for me, the people took a real risk. Yesterday, I knifed Roman soldiers. But tomorrow I might do the same to a fellow Jew. People knew that since I worship the god of power, I might turn against them at any time. So in asking for me, the people did take some risk.

However, how long do you think terrorists really last? The people who asked for me knew that either I'd try another suicide raid, and some Roman mercenary would mark up another one on his sword, or one of my own kind would do me in. Either way, I would soon be forgotten, and nobody would see who the real enemy is.

It makes sense to believe that the enemy is out there — the hated Romans who control our country; Herod, the half-Jew "king," who liked Roman money; or the "sinners," who refused to go along with the Moral Majority Pharisees. Even though I was a killer, I supported the illusion that the enemy is somewhere *out there*.

But the Nazarene said just the opposite. He said the real enemy is *within us*. The Nazarene said that when God calls to us, we hide behind our fig leaves of religion. Rather than to risk coming before God empty-handed, we either trot out our parents' religion, or complain that they made us go to church. But one fig leaf is as phony as the other. Instead of appealing to religion or offering excuses, God invites us to see his call, "Where are you?" (Genesis 3:9), as friendly. Even though *we* are the enemy, God invites us to believe that he sees us as his friend.

But ever since the Fall, people have been hearing "other voices." We keep confusing who the enemy is. We think God is the enemy, or that the enemy is *out there*. But the enemy is always in here — in us. The Nazarene called us to see that, and went a dangerous step further. He said, "I am the friendly voice of God asking, 'Where are you?' "

Whether people think they are religious or not, they always try to silence that voice. That's why people choose me instead of him. I didn't show them who the real enemy is. I supported the illusion that the enemy is *out there*.

People choose me instead of Jesus, because I am a safe terrorist. I don't really require anything new of people, and I keep people from seeing who the real enemy is.

I might try to sound tough, or to look threatening, but
am a safe terrorist. Jesus is the dangerous one,
sus is the one who can really change your life, who,
re-arrange this world more than my little sword.

But at some point in life you must decide

There are risks in following either of us

To be like me, or to follow Jesus, is a real risk. But, Unlike myself, Jesus has much to give; and he is fighting a holy war against
the real enemy. So . . . why/me, instead of him?

the only one who can

us change

choose

He requires something very new

Following him will mean making
a lot of changes;

<table>
<tr><td rowspan="3" style="font-size:2em">6</td><td><h1>MARY</h1></td></tr>
<tr><td>Faith At</td></tr>
<tr><td>The Cross</td></tr>
</table>

Order of Worship

CALL TO WORSHIP

Leader: We meet here in the name of God — Father, Son, and Holy Spirit.

People: These words remind us of our Baptism, in which we were marked with the Cross of Christ.

Leader: The Cross of Christ reminds us that the rebellion which began in the Garden of Eden, and which we have repeated, must be condemned.

People: The Cross of Christ also means that we are never alone in our suffering, that God stands with the condemned.

Leader: Yet, rather than risk the pain of the Cross, we hold fellowship hours before and after church, and we use God's money for air conditioning and pew cushions.

People: Rather than struggle with God ourselves, we let the hard work be done by Bible experts or theological committees.

Leader: Rather than admit and struggle with our feelings of hurt, anger, and fear, we put up a false front of confidence and peace.

People: Instead of looking for support within the fellowship of the Cross, we chase illusions in hard work, recreation, or self-help books.

46

All: *Lord God, give us your Spirit, that we may stand at the Cross, be comforted in our pain, and with bold faith follow where you lead us. Amen*

HYMN

THE SCRIPTURE LESSON   John 19:23-27

THE LENTEN MESSAGE   *Mary — Faith at the Cross*

A RESPONSIVE PRAYER OF FAITH

Leader: Lord God, help us to see that in our Baptism, we started to walk in the way of Christ's Cross.

People: Help us to see when we, instead of following you, try to take comfortable detours.

Leader: Give us your Spirit, that in all of our suffering, we may see that you are with us.

People: Lead us out of all our illusions and self-help projects to the support of the fellowship of the Cross.

Leader: Give us a strong and humble faith in all of your promises.

People: Lord God, whatever our feelings, help us to say and live, "We belong to you. Have your way with us!"

HYMN

PRAYERS

THE OFFERING

THE DISMISSAL

Leader: Live joyfully and gratefully, by the power of the Holy Spirit, as you share in Christ's Cross and in his resurrection. In the midst of your pain and doubts, cling to faith in God's promises!

People: We do trust God's promises, and even when we can't, we still stand with each other!

Suggested Hymns: "Lift High the Cross"
"He's Everything to Me"
"In the Cross of Christ I Glory"

Mary — Faith at the Cross

A Monolog

When I heard that Yeshua was to be crucified, I wanted to be there with him. Although it was like a knife in my heart, I had to support him to the very end. I am Mary, his mother.

Even before John came to tell me that Yeshua had been condemned to death, I felt the bitter truth of what Simeon had long ago said. When Joseph and I had taken Yeshua to the Temple to present him to the Lord, Simeon, a complete stranger, had shocked us by taking our baby into his arms and saying that the Lord would use him to save the world. Then Simeon told me, "This child is set for the fall and rising of many in Israel, and for a sign that is spoken against . . . that thoughts out of many hearts may be revealed." I could hardly imagine the Son of the Most High being spoken against. But Simeon had touched my shoulder and sighed, "And a sword will pierce through your own soul also." (Luke 2:34-35)

When I saw many people run after my son only for what they could get from him; when I saw the jealousy and hatred of most of our spiritual leaders against my son, it really hurt. I knew that our people had a long history of stubborn rebellion against God and his prophets, but I'd always hoped it would somehow be different with my son.

I remember the day when I was told that I would be his mother. I was cleaning a neighbor's house. I had just said a quick prayer for Israel's freedom, when a shaft of light through a lattice window caught my eye. The light seemed to take on human form. I thought I was seeing things, when a voice said, "God bless you, dear Mary! The Lord is with you. No woman has ever lived on earth to whom God has shown such grace!" "I don't feel very privileged," I said to myself. "I'm just an orphan girl, working in a little village that's not even mentioned in the Bible. Me — the most fortunate woman alive?"

I must have looked confused and scared, because the voice said, "Don't be afraid, Mary. For you have found favor with God and, hear this! You shall conceive a child and give birth to a son. And you shall name him Yeshua. He will be great and called the Son of the Most High. And the Lord will give him the throne of his father

David, and he will rule over the house of Jacob forever. And of his kingdom there shall be no end.''

When I heard the part about having a baby — before I could stop myself — I said out loud, ''But how can that happen since I'm not married?'' The voice said it would be just as it was at the first creation — the Holy Spirit would hover over me, and the Owner of heaven and earth would cause his Son to be formed in me.

The hard part wasn't that God would conceive my baby. After all, I believe that God can do anything! I just couldn't believe this was happening to me. Why would God choose a nobody like me? I didn't know what I was saying when I blurted out, ''I belong to the Lord. May it happen to me as you have said.''

As Yeshua grew up, and Joseph and I had children of our own, it seemed less clear to me what God had in mind for him. Yeshua shocked us that time in the Temple — when he was twelve; but, otherwise he was a normal teen-ager and young adult. He worked with Joseph in his carpenter shop. Since he was maybe a better craftsman than Joseph, we hoped he might set up his own shop.

I was surprised when Yeshua became a traveling rabbi. Although I encouraged him, I worried about how he'd support himself. The usual custom was that if a Jewish man wanted to study under a rabbi, he first had to get the rabbi's permission. Instead, my son went around Galilee selecting students himself. And some of his choices worried me — even if a number of his followers were our own relatives!

I always believed my son was the world's savior, but he scared me when he talked about his ''hour.'' I always thought the Day of the Lord was when God himself would appear on earth to destroy all his enemies, and to reward faithful Israel with all of the world's blessings. We Galileans, who had seen the Assyrians, the Babylonians, the Greeks, and the Romans plunder our land, especially longed for the Day of the Lord. But my son had a strangely different view. He talked instead about the Day of Atonement, when the Scapegoat, upon whom the sins of the people had been laid, was then sent out to the wilderness, never to return to the camp. He talked about Isaiah's Suffering Servant, the innocent one offered up as a sacrifice for the nations. When I urged him to reveal who he really was, Yeshua would get a distant look in his eyes, and say, ''My hour is not yet come!'' When he talked like that, my son seemed like a stranger to me.

Among his followers, I felt very close to John, Zebedee's son, partly because John was my favorite nephew, but mostly because he alone seemed to share my feelings about Yeshua. John seemed to look beyond the strange things Yeshua said and did. He seemed to know who Yeshua really was. John would often tell me about my son's shocking speeches, and we spent hours talking about what Yeshua meant.

After my son rode into Jerusalem as if he were the king, and made that scene in the Temple — throwing out the sacrifice peddlers and the money-changers — I knew the house of Annas would soon strike back. Annas had always been afraid to arrest my son, because he knew the people thought my son was such a great hero. But when Yeshua rode into Jerusalem — clearly saying he *was* Israel's *true* King — Annas and his puppet son-in-law, Caiaphas, knew they had to get rid of him. When I warned my son that Annas was plotting to kill him, Yeshua said, "My hour is not yet come." Since I didn't know where he was most of that Passover week at night, I thought Yeshua meant he would not let the authorities capture him.

I couldn't believe it that Friday morning when John came to my house with tears in his eyes and told me about my son's secret arrest the night before. He said he and Simon Peter had followed to the High Priest's house, and he had listened to most of the hearing there. He said I should be proud of how my son had handled himself. He said Yeshua stood silently while all the twisted garbage was dug up against him. "Why was he condemned?" I asked John. My nephew got a pained look on his face. I took both his hands and said, "I have to know, John. Did Yeshua say who he really is?" John looked away from me and spoke slowly, "He said, so all could hear, that he is the Lord's Anointed One, and that we will see him seated at the right hand of Power, and coming on the clouds of heaven." John said our Supreme Council had immediately ruled such talk is blasphemy. He said they turned Yeshua over to Pontius Pilate, who had no choice but to pass the death sentence against my son.

Although I felt as if my own life were over, I seemed strangely at peace. My son's "hour" had finally come. He had revealed himself as the true Israel, God's Servant; but he would be enthroned as the Scapegoat, the one upon whom the people's sins were laid, who was then cast out of the camp forever. This was a terrible reality for me to face.

But, even in our tears, John and I knew what we had to do. Despite the fact that we could be arrested also, we had to go to Skull Hill and be with Yeshua. We didn't understand my son's "hour," but it had come, as he said it would, and we had to be there with him.

When I saw my son's bruised body, and listened to the taunts of his enemies, and the crude talk of the execution detachment, it seemed like a terrible dream. I kept hoping that I would wake up, and find out that it wasn't true. But I knew it was.

I was mad at myself for believing who my son was, and for urging him to follow his dreams, so he could die like a common criminal at the hands of cruel people who were supposed to be our spiritual leaders! I cried out that it was unfair. Worse yet, it all seemed so hopeless now.

I'm so glad that John was there. He let me rage and cry. He just stood by and held me in his strong arms. There wasn't anything he could do or say.

I knew that my son's "hour" had come — that I would have to give him up. He nodded toward John, and said quietly to me, in his usual way, "Woman, he is now your son!" And with a look that only John could understand, he said to him, "She is now your mother!"

Although "the sword pierced my soul," as Simeon had said it would, I felt strangely privileged. I didn't understand it all; but the Rule of God I believed, had touched the earth, and God's Son had walked among us. I didn't know what the Most High was up to, but I felt his presence as never before that day — and it was a lasting presence.

Looking at my son's broken body — and at the strangely dark sky — and feeling the earth shake beneath me, I heard myself saying what I had said when my son was conceived, "I belong to the Lord. May it happen to me as you have said!"

<table>
<tr><td>7</td><td># JESUS

A Service For
Maundy Thursday</td></tr>
</table>

Order of Worship

CALL TO WORSHIP

Leader: We meet here in the name of God — Father, Son, and Holy Spirit.

People: Like the first disciples, we recognize Jesus in the breaking of the bread, and he becomes present with and through us.

Leader: In the Lord's Supper, we remember that God passes over our sins and sets us free from the power of sin and death.

People: In the Lord's Supper, we are caught up in God's mighty act of rescue. God assures us that our sins are forgiven, and that we are his special people.

All: Until Christ returns, we proclaim his death, and make him present in what we say and do.

HYMN

SCRIPTURE LESSON Exodus 12:1-13

THE LENTEN MESSAGE *Remember Me!*

A REFLECTION UPON THE PASSOVER AND THE LORD'S SUPPER

54

Leader: The Passover meal recalls Israel's great independence day — escape from slavery and death in Egypt.

People: The Lord's Supper recalls our being set free from the power of sin and death.

Leader: In the Passover, the Jewish believer receives his identity and gains hope for the future.

People: In the Lord's Supper, we recall our adoption into God's family and renew our hope that nothing can separate us from God.

Leader: We receive Communion, not to get our sins forgiven, but to be assured that they are forgiven.

People: The question in the Lord's Supper is not, "Who should be allowed to commune?" but "Do we need to repent from our sins?" and "Do we need God's forgiveness?"

Leader: The Jewish Passover was a family affair. It was part of a meal and everyone had a part in that celebration.

People: The Lord's Supper is a family affair, too. It can be celebrated anywhere and any believer may consecrate the bread and wine for our common use.

Leader: In the Lord's Supper, the main question is not, "How is Christ present?"

People: The main question is "Will we make Christ present *in our meetings and in our everyday lives?"'*

All: Lord God, pass over all those who repent and trust in you; and move us out to occupy the world for you — until you return to end the age. Amen

THE OFFERING AND PRESENTATION OF BREAD AND WINE

THE WORDS OF INSTITUTION

THE DISTRIBUTION OF HOLY COMMUNION

HYMN

THE DISMISSAL

Leader: Live joyfully and faithfully, in the power of the Holy Spirit, as you share in Christ's death and resurrection. In the midst of human affairs, be a witness for Christ.

People: **As a set-apart, gifted people, we leave this place, made special by God's Word, to make Christ present where we live, work, and play.**

Suggested Hymns: "Sons of God, Hear His Holy Word"
"Let Us Break Bread Together"
"Sent Forth by God's Blessing"

Jesus — Remember Me!

A Monolog

I gave you my Supper, but I'm amazed at what's happened to its meaning and practice. Some of my followers say that the bread and wine are really me. Some say the bread and wine are to remind people of me. Some say that each time the bread and wine are set aside for my Supper, I am sacrificed again for the sins of the world. I'm amazed that my followers don't seem to have caught what I said two times: *Remember* me!

I know that during their common meal, some of my early followers made fools of themselves. Some got drunk and others wouldn't share their food. So my ambassador Paul suggested that my followers in Corinth eat their meals at home and then share my Supper when they met together. But I wonder why Paul's suggestion got set in concrete, and hardly anyone today shares my Supper during a common meal together! When I gave my Supper, I wonder if anybody was listening to what I said: *Remember* me!

One reason why people don't understand my Supper is they don't study the Passover very carefully. For my people Israel, the Passover meal was not a time when the family got together and said, "Let's talk about the good ol' days when God acted to save our ancestors." It's true that the Passover was to be celebrated in a set way. The younger children were supposed to ask questions about why certain foods were being used. And the family leader rehearsed the answers that the older children and adults already knew (Exodus 12:25-27)

But the Passover wasn't just a rehashing of the past. Celebrating the Passover involved people in the Exodus. The Passover celebration changed the present, and gave hope for the future. Listen to what is written in the scroll of Deuteronomy: "When your son asks you in time to come, 'What is the meaning of the testimonies and the statutes and the ordinances which the Lord our God had commanded you?' then you shall say to your son, '*We* were Pharaoh's slaves in Egypt; and the Lord brought *us* out of Egypt with a mighty hand; and the Lord showed signs and wonders . . . against Egypt and against Pharaoh and all his household, before *our* eyes; and he brought *us* out from there, that he might bring us in and give *us* the land which he swore to give to our fathers.' " (Deuteronomy 6:20-23)

The Passover is not just a story about what happened to our ancestors. We are involved in the Exodus. "*We* were slaves in Egypt . . . and the Lord brought *us* out . . . that he might bring *us* in and give *us* the land" which he promised to give our ancestors. The Passover celebration made the Exodus present again. It gave my people their identity and moved them out to occupy the promised land for God — it's rightful owner. The Passover isn't just thinking about the past. It is a celebration that changes the present and gives my people hope for the future.

It was during a Passover meal that I started a new celebration. After I had given thanks, I took some of the small pieces of bread, which reminded my people of their smallness in Egypt, I broke the bread, and said, "This is me! I will be made small, I will be broken for you!" Later, when the time came to share the traditional cup of blessing, I said, "This cup is the new covenant in my blood, which is poured out for many for the forgiveness of sins."

The Passover meal celebrated my people's escape from slavery and death in Egypt. It made my people who they are, and gave them hope during times of foreign occupation. It reminded us that our world is really under God's control.

But the human tragedy is not a matter of physical oppression, of regulating the economy, or of healing diseases. The human tragedy is that people are separated from God, separated from each other, and separated from whom they really are. The enemy is not Egypt, Babylonia, or Rome — some foreign power. The enemy is spiritual, called Devil and Satan. The enemy is within us — our refusal to let God decide what is good for us and what is not good for us.

My role is to bring God and people back together. Unlike Adam and every one of his children, I let God decide what is good for me and what is not good for me. I lived out what Moses told a new generation in the Sinai desert: "Man doesn't live by bread alone, but by every word that God speaks." What kept me going was my desire to do God's will. I am the Second Adam — what God created people to be and to do.

I also see myself as the Scapegoat, the one goat upon whom the High Priest lays the sins of the people, and who is then led out into the wilderness, there to wander and die, so that the people may come into God's presence. As the Scriptures say, there can be no forgiveness — people can't be untied, unloosed from their sins — without the shedding of blood. I offer my innocent life so that people everywhere may be welcomed back into God's family, and into acceptance with each other.

Because of my obedience, my trust, and my sacrifice, God now looks at people in a new way. God sees, not the sin of Adam, but my obedience and faith. Because of what I have done, God has cancelled the death sentence against the world, and he welcomes all people back into his family again. My role is to bring God and people back together, to be a human bridge to right relationships — with God, with each other, and with yourself.

The Passover brought freedom and new life only to my people Israel. All other races of people need a Passover, too. That's why I called my Supper "the New Covenant." Through my life and death, God reached out to the whole world in a new way. That was why God had chosen Abram — that all races of people might be blessed through him. I am Abraham's promised Descendant, the New Israel, the Lord's Servant to all the nations.

Neither the covenant with Abraham nor the New Covenant is an agreement between equals. The Covenant is an offer from God to people who cannot and do not deserve it. The Covenant, whether Old or New, is an undeserved *gift*!

Some of my followers seem to forget that. Some say you have to agree to a certain set of teachings, or to a certain kind of authority structure, before you can receive my Supper. They forget that I shared my Supper with Judas, the son of the Devil, who betrayed me, and with Peter, who told the mob he didn't even know me! My Supper isn't for a select, deserving few. It is for everyone who is willing to turn from their sin, and accept me as their Savior.

No special person is needed to make me present in my Supper. I made every one of you my special Ambassador, my Witness, when you were baptized. Any one of you can set apart bread and wine for the faith community to proclaim my death until I return in victory to end the age.

Reciting what I said when I gave my Supper doesn't make me present. I am present with my followers when they recognize that they belong to me, and to each other. That was the problem in Corinth. Folks there would only listen to and support their favorite preacher, and they wouldn't share what they had with each other. They said all the right words, but they didn't make me present in their meetings, or in their lives. They limited my Spirit to their favorite preacher, and they decided who deserved their help. I can't be present in a group like that! Even if they recite the words of institution, that group does not ''Remember me!'' That kind of group is not celebrating my Supper.

In my Supper, the question is not, ''How am I present?'' or ''Who makes me present?'' If you recognize that you belong to my Body, and that you exist for the sake of people who need you, then you ''Remember me,'' then you celebrate my Supper.

When I said in my Supper, ''Do this to remember me,'' I meant more than ''think about me.'' In my Supper, I call you to recognize whom you belong to, and because you are mine, you are to share yourself with those who need you. Then I am present — for you and through you. Remember me! Remember that I am for you; when you come to your senses, you can always come home to God. Make me present again as you offer yourself to people who have gotten lost, and who need you. Then you have a true Lord's Supper. Then you will have remembered me!